30 Minutes
... To Manage
Information
Overload

30 Minutes
... To Manage Information Overload

John Caunt

**KOGAN
PAGE**

Kogan Page Limited
120 Pentonville Road
London N1 9JN

© John Caunt, 1999

British Library Cataloguing in Publication Data
A CIP record for this book is available from the British Library.

ISBN 0 7494 2980 1

Typeset by The Florence Group, Stoodleigh, Devon

Printed and bound by Clays Ltd, St Ives plc

CONTENTS

The 30 Minutes Series

The *Kogan Page 30 Minutes Series* has been devised to give your confidence a boost when faced with tackling a new skill or challenge for the first time.

So the next time you're thrown in at the deep end and want to bring your skills up to scratch or pep up your career prospects, turn to the *30 Minutes Series* for help!

Titles available are:

30 Minutes Before a Meeting

30 Minutes Before Your Job Appraisal

30 Minutes Before Your Job Interview

30 Minutes To Boost Your Communication Skills

30 Minutes To Brainstorm Great Ideas

30 Minutes To Get Your Own Way

30 Minutes To Make the Right Decision

30 Minutes To Make the Right Impression

30 Minutes To Market Yourself

30 Minutes To Master the Internet

30 Minutes To Motivate Your Staff

30 Minutes To Plan a Project

30 Minutes To Prepare a Job Application

30 Minutes To Succeed in Business Writing

30 Minutes To Write a Business Plan

30 Minutes To Write a Marketing Plan

30 Minutes To Write a Report

30 Minutes To Write Sales Letters

Available from all good booksellers.
For further information on the series, please contact:

Kogan Page, 120 Pentonville Road, London N1 9JN
Tel: 0171 278 0433 Fax: 0171 837 6348

INTRODUCTION

Information overload is today's workplace epidemic. In all countries throughout the developed world, and in all walks of life, people are struggling to assimilate and deal with the vast quantities of information they are required to handle in their jobs. Various surveys have pointed to widespread stress, loss of job satisfaction and productivity decline as a direct result of information overload. And it is not getting any easier. While some organizations are making efforts to reduce the volume of information presented and stored on paper, the amount of electronic communication continues to escalate. The teetering in-tray may be replaced by the log-jammed e-mail in-box, but electronic communication is not always easier to deal with, and is more prone to overuse. Increased volumes of information have been brought about by:

- greater public and industry-specific regulation;
- growth of multiple-location organizations and global competition;

● technology that allows information to be generated, stored and transported with increasing ease.

There is little we can do as individuals to halt the global tide, but most of us are in a position to manage our own corner a little better and to influence those who work with us. In so doing, we can become more productive and less stressed. That is the purpose of this book. In 30 minutes it aims to introduce you to techniques and strategies that will help you to beat information overload.

WHAT DO WE DO WITH INFORMATION?

In simple terms we may identify five types of action we take with information:

1. We create it (writing letters, memos, reports, e-mails; preparing statistics, charts, presentations).

2. We communicate it (sending and receiving by paper, phone, fax, e-mail, or face to face).

3. We interpret it (reading and understanding material).

4. We manipulate or act upon it (using it to inform plans, decisions and responses; combining it with other information; summarizing or re-presenting it for others).

5. We store or discard it (computer file, filing cabinet, memory or bin).

The effective management of information overload requires attention to all the above, and to interactions with other people and with technology. Before we move on to consider these, take a moment to ask yourself what type of information problems you suffer from.

INFORMATION OVERLOAD – THE SYMPTOMS

Here are some symptoms of information overload:

1. I don't have time to read material that is sent for my attention.

2. I am not satisfied with my ability to keep up with developments in my area of work.

3. I am seldom able to clear my in-tray.

4. I don't often tackle paperwork when I first look at it.

5. I have difficulty finding documents I need to work on.

6. My colleagues bombard me with information I don't need.

7. I haven't time to sort out my personal files.

8. Interruptions prevent me concentrating on information-intensive tasks.

9. I am plagued by junk mail, fax and e-mail.

10. I am concerned that I am not adequately utilizing technology in managing information.

11. I am often unable to decide what to do with documents I receive.

12. I wish I could assimilate documents more quickly.

13. I am often unsure whether I have amassed the best available information to carry out a task.

14. I forget a lot of what I read.

15. I can't find what I want on the Internet.

16. The sheer volume of information I have to handle just keeps on rising.

If none of the above apply to you, then you have probably picked up the wrong book, but if you recognize your
situation, read on.

PUT YOURSELF IN CONTROL

The rest of this book is about putting yourself in control
of information. It should be there to work for you – your
servant, not your master. Putting yourself in control means
separating the vital from the marginal, treasuring the
former and dumping the latter. It means recognizing your
current weaknesses in handling information and working
to remove them; and it means knowing that we can only
use information effectively if it is accessible when we need
it, understandable and reliable.

1

CHANGE YOUR INFORMATION HABITS

ELIMINATE NEGATIVE HABITS

Information overload is like congestion on the roads. When we find ourselves slowed to a crawl by the weight of traffic, we curse the other drivers, but fail to acknowledge that we are also part of the problem. The first step in managing the problem is, then, to look at ourselves, and identify the negative work habits which fuel information overload.

Fear lies at the heart of many negative information handling habits:

- fear of being held accountable for failures in communication;

- fear of appearing stupid;

- fear of missing or losing an important piece of information.

These fears lead us to communicate the unnecessary, hang on to the worthless and search after information perfection. Here are three examples.

Over-copying

Over-copying is a form of workplace insurance. When you're not sure what to do with a document or who may need sight of a memo, the easiest solution is to run off multiple copies and send them to everybody who might conceivably have use for the information therein. You have achieved two things – the offending item is off your desk, and you have also absolved yourself from any responsibility for failure to communicate. However, you have added to the information burden of others and have not necessarily communicated anything. If you aim to protect yourself by over-copying to colleagues, they are likely to respond in the same way.

Over-research

When faced with the production of a report or presentation, you engage in research and information gathering out of proportion with the task in hand. The result is that you become bogged down with data, unable to see the wood for the trees, and the finished article suffers accordingly. At other times you relentlessly plough through documents of only passing significance out of concern that somewhere within them might be an essential nugget of information, and you put items to one side telling yourself that you will read them at some illusory time when you are 'not quite so busy'.

Procrastination

Few objects in our working lives are more stressful than the sight of a full in-tray, whether it be of the traditional or electronic variety. The most common approach is to tackle the easy items first and to put aside for later consideration those that require more work, thought or energy. Some element of postponement is both inevitable and necessary in a busy work schedule, but we give ourselves needless stress and reduce our effectiveness if we indulge in habitual procrastination. We present ourselves with excuses such as:

- 'I haven't got all the information I need to tackle this job.'

- 'I don't have time at the moment to do it justice.'

- 'There are other deadlines which are more pressing.'

- 'If I do nothing with this, it will probably go away.'

We tackle the easier items and those with tight deadlines while tasks which may be among the most important remain undone. But the stress of not tackling a particular task is often greater than that involved in carrying it out. We waste time and energy worrying about the things we have not done when with a little more resolve they could be consigned to the out-tray.

Putting tasks off to another day is not the only problem. Just as prevalent is the tendency to delay getting down to the main job in hand by using minor tasks as self-imposed diversions. This is very time and energy destructive. With a little self-discipline it can be overcome.

Strategies for beating procrastination

- Own up to it. Recognizing that the problem exists is the first step to overcoming it.

- Discriminate between the routine and the difficult tasks and give the latter priority on your 'to do' lists.

- Schedule times in your diary for tackling tasks you don't like.

- Force yourself to spend a set period of time before you will allow yourself a break.

- Note the frequency with which tasks turn out to be less fearsome than expected. Use this knowledge as a reference to help overcome future anxieties.

- Reward yourself for removing difficult tasks from the pile.

- Divide large tasks into bite-sized chunks in order to make it easier to get started on a project.

- When you have broken down a project, pitch in at whatever stage is the easiest to get the task underway.

- Set your own deadlines for tasks where they are not externally imposed.

NURTURE POSITIVE INFORMATION HABITS

Identify what is important

Some information is immediately recognizable as junk. Other items scream their importance. But it isn't always simple to separate with certainty the vital from the marginal. You give yourself a better chance of doing so if you are clear about the key responsibilities and objectives in your job, and are able to use them as a form of mental checklist against which you can match whatever information comes your way.

You cannot be sure of getting it right every time, but resist the temptation to deal with this uncertainty by a strategy of 'if in doubt, treat it as important'. Remember that information perfection – always having exactly the right information available at the right time – is not possible. While the availability of good information is important to the effective discharge of your job, more information will not guarantee better performance. Beyond a certain point, additional information will have a declining marginal value, and information has no value at all if there is so much of it that it cannot be properly interpreted and understood. So recognize that you have no hope of taking in everything, focus on the important and accept that your judgement will be imperfect.

You will also need to discriminate between the urgent and the important. Items requiring a speedy response may assume a greater importance than they deserve. An unimportant matter that has been left unattended for several days does not become any more important because its deadline is approaching. It simply becomes more urgent.

Adopt a systematic approach towards information received

There is a common myth, perpetuated by some time management programmes, that every piece of paper should be handled only once. It doesn't work like that in the real world. For a variety of reasons, you might need to come back to a document. An item may genuinely need to be mulled over or put together with other information before you can make a sensible decision upon it. It may be more efficient to deal with some items in context with others on the same subject. What about the document that makes you angry? Although a response fired off immediately is personally satisfying, it may be more effective to wait a couple of days and respond with cool logic. Some items may need repeated handling in the process of drafting a complex document.

If it is possible to touch a document only once, then this is clearly what you should aim for, but don't become too hung up on the 'one touch' approach. Ensure that no document goes back onto the pile, and that every item receives a positive action on the first touch. This action should be one of the following five Ds:

1. Discard it.
2. Deal with it.
3. Determine a future action.
4. Direct or distribute it.
5. Deposit it.

1. **Discard it**: the quickest way to become bogged down with information is by wasting time and energy reading material of little or no benefit to your work. So, the first question to ask yourself is 'Do I want this at all?' It should be quickly apparent if an item has no use for you, but we are often reluctant to consider the bin until we have waded through a document. There is also a tendency to put to one side documents that one is unsure about. There they form a mounting pile with other items, gathering dust and occasionally being revisited in half-hearted attempts to clear the backlog. Remember that most information has a limited shelf life. A useful rule of thumb is – if it doesn't seem valuable today it isn't likely to tomorrow.

2. **Deal with it**: an immediate action on a document is satisfying and stress-relieving. It also means that you will not have to spend time refreshing your memory before you can act upon it in the future. Where it is not possible to deal with an item immediately, then at least determine what action you will take and when.

3. **Determine a future action**: never return an item to the pile. Make sure you have a system for bringing forward items on which you will need to act, and make a point of noting the action required, or the possible options, on the document or a sticky note attachment. A concertina file marked with the dates of the month makes a useful 'bring forward' device. Place the item in the compartment corresponding to the date when you wish to revisit it. Use project files for items that need to be worked upon with others as part of a larger task.

You will need to exert some discipline in respect of items determined for future action:

- Do not use it to avoid one of the other four Ds.

- Do not move items on beyond the day you have originally set for action.

- If you have a 'to read' file, don't let it become a general dumping ground.

4. **Direct or distribute it**: don't send items to others just to get them off your own desk or because you don't know what to do with them. You will only add to other people's information burden, further belabour the internal communication system and possibly fill the bins of others more quickly than your own. Think about why you are redirecting the item and what you want the other person to do with it. A brief note will help them to assimilate and act upon it more quickly.

5. **Deposit it**: storing an item in whatever form of filing system is not an action to take because you don't know what else to do with it. Be sparing in what you file. We will look at ground rules for filing a little later.

2

DEVELOP YOUR INFORMATION HANDLING SKILLS

READ MORE EFFICIENTLY

It has been estimated that people in information-intensive jobs may spend a third of their working day in activities involving reading, and yet most of us are not as efficient readers as we might be. The average reading speed is between 200 and 250 words a minute. With some simple techniques and practice this can easily be raised to 500+ without detriment to your understanding. Slow reading speeds are not particularly a function of education or intelligence. Many able and well-educated people read at or below the average speed. Even if you already read quickly, there is generally scope for improvement. It is a myth that only by reading slowly can we expect to understand material. Better comprehension can go hand in hand with faster reading.

Why do we read slowly?

When we read, our eyes do not move continuously across the page, but rather hop several words at a time through the material. It is during the stationary period (fixation) at the end of each hop that the reading occurs; and it is, of course, the brain that does the reading rather than the eyes. In simple terms, we might think of the eyes as a still camera taking a series of shots which the brain then interprets. The main reasons for slow reading speed are:

- limited number of words encompassed in each fixation;

- fixations of longer duration than necessary;

- involuntary or deliberate back skipping over material already read.

A fourth factor in slow reading is a tendency to mentally hear the words as we read. This is known as sub-vocalization and is believed to originate from the approach used when we first learn to read – actually speaking the words aloud. The problem with sub-vocalization is that it restricts us to little more than the speed of the spoken voice, which is typically around 150 words a minute. Sub-vocalization can be greatly diminished if never entirely eliminated.

Training yourself to read faster is a matter of technique and practice. There are numerous books and courses available on the subject, and in the space available here, it is only possible to introduce a few techniques. With a little determination, these should bring about a significant improvement.

Using a pacer

Most speed reading programmes advocate training with some form of pacing technique which forces your eyes to move on and eliminates lengthy pauses or back skipping.

You can use your index finger or the blunt end of a pencil, moving it swiftly across the page just below the line of text you are reading. At the end of the line, move the pacer quickly to the start of the next line, and so on. Maintain a pace above that which feels comfortable and refuse to allow your eyes to go back over what you have already read. At first you may feel that you have taken in little or nothing of what your eyes have passed over, but with practice you will find increased levels of comprehension as well as speed. It has been shown that faster readers actually understand more because they are able to tune in to the general thrust of the piece they are reading, whereas slower readers become bogged down in detail.

It is natural to feel some anxiety about the process of taking in larger blocks of material at each hit, but in many aspects of our daily lives we absorb significant blocks of information at a glance. We register road signs, hoardings and headlines without stopping to 'read' them and we can significantly increase the span of words that we take in on each fixation. It is commonly thought that fast readers read down the middle of the page and that their span therefore encompasses the whole line of text. This is, however, very difficult to achieve except with text in columns. Fast readers may take in six or more words per fixation, and their eyes will remain in the central third of the page rather than following a line down the centre of it.

As your reading speed increases, you should find yourself able to progress to a smooth zigzag movement of the pacer, taking in more than one line at each pass, and without the necessity to lift the pacer from the page. Avoid reaching the point where you are forcing yourself along and are more conscious of the process of reading quickly than of what you are taking in. Once you have reached a reasonable speed you may wish to relinquish your pacer.

Other techniques

Increasing your reading speed will, of course, take a little time and you may wish to tap into the structured practice of a speed reading course. Whether or not you choose to do so, here are some further techniques you can employ almost immediately to improve both speed and understanding.

Preview for increased understanding

We read much more quickly and effectively if we are slotting information into a known framework. A few moments spent establishing that framework can pay significant dividends. The approach which follows assumes you are setting out to read a substantial document such as a book, periodical or report. It can be adapted for shorter documents:

1. Before starting on the main text, skim through the Contents page, Introduction and Summary (if there is one) or Conclusions.

2. Next, flick through the document, establishing an appreciation of the main structure and argument. Look particularly for section or chapter summaries. They are excellent for getting quickly to the guts of a document. Failing that, read the first and last paragraph of each section or chapter. These will often introduce and summarize the arguments contained therein.

3. Now, when you move to read the document properly, you will be filling in the gaps rather than starting with a blank sheet. You will know which are the parts you need to concentrate on, and which you can blast through or skip altogether.

Vary your pace

It goes without saying that text varies in its level of difficulty, but many people maintain the same pace regardless of what they are reading. Even within a document there will be some sections that are more difficult to absorb than others. Don't be afraid to slow down where the text requires it, and to power through the easier passages.

Focus on what is important

At some point in most documents there will be digressions from the main argument, things which you already know, things you don't need to know and straightforward padding. The best way to approach any reading task is with the question 'What do I need from this?' foremost in your mind. You will read more quickly and remember more if you can focus on the elements that are necessary for you in whatever task you have to fulfil. Don't approach the printed word with too much reverence. The writer does not necessarily know any more than you do on the subject.

Get the environment right

Your reading efficiency is affected by your surroundings and feelings. Ensure that lighting is adequate and distractions are minimized. Significant amounts of reading from computer screens is particularly wearing, so take care to adjust the contrast and brightness for maximum comfort and take more frequent breaks than you would with paper-work.

Develop scanning techniques

When you need to find a particular piece of information, you can move to it quickly by scanning. Focus your attention solely on the information you wish to locate and let your eyes follow your finger as you run it rapidly down the centre of each page from top to bottom. This process should be considerably faster than your paced reading, and if you are focused on the information you want to locate, it should leap out at you when you get to the relevant part of the document. You will improve with practice. Of course, scanning is no substitute for using an index where one exists.

IMPROVE CONCENTRATION

The ability to concentrate is vital to successful management of a heavy information load, but for many it is a perennial weak spot. The strategies you can adopt to maintain and improve concentration include:

- scheduling particular times for those activities that require a high level of concentration;

- recognizing that there will be certain times of the day when your levels of concentration are higher. These will vary from person to person – all our body rhythms are different. There may also be times of the working week when your ability to concentrate is lower. For example, accumulated fatigue may mean that Friday afternoons are low concentration times.

- ensuring that your immediate environment is conducive to concentration. It should be as free as possible of external distractions and interruptions.

- taking frequent short breaks to avoid fatigue. Don't let yourself be distracted into another activity during the breaks, and be firm about their timing and duration.

- setting yourself clear goals in every work session.

USE YOUR MEMORY

The value of information declines pretty rapidly if we can't remember it. Fear of forgetting results in a number of negative habits. We hang on to documents of minor significance, read slowly and back skip over the printed page. For effective information handling we need to trust our memories. The more we use them, the more reliable they will be. If you do nothing to assist your memory you will forget up to 80 per cent of what you read within 24 hours of reading it. There are a number of simple techniques that can help you remember better.

The level of recall you require will vary. For some information, it will be sufficient for you to remember simply that it exists and where to find it. With other information you will need a grasp of the general subject and main ideas. At the highest level you may need to recall information in detail or even verbatim. Assist your memory by selective reading and awareness of the level of recall you need.

Read with a question in your mind. What do I want to achieve from this? How does it fit into what I know already? All learning and remembering is a process of association.

Try to see the overall pattern to what you are reading. We remember much better if we can see the general structure and the broad ideas into which the detail fits.

Use the information in some way. Summarize it in your own words, make margin notes as you read, communicate the information to others, or act on it.

Recognition, the process of remembering with assistance from an external stimulus, is much easier than pure recall. Make conscious associations which will help you to pull detail from your memory. It has been shown that the more bizarre the association, the more likely it is to work. Silly mnemonics, ridiculous visual associations, they all work.

Review important information up to four times to fix it in your long-term memory. The optimum times for review are: approximately 10 minutes after acquiring the information; after a day; after a week; and after a month.

3

CONQUER THE PAPER MOUNTAIN

REDUCE INFLOW

However effective you become at handling the stuff, you will not achieve all that is possible unless you also take steps to reduce the volume of paper which daily arrives on your desk. Even if you only glance at the majority of it, you may be wasting considerable time and effort:

- Don't invite junk mail by handing out your business cards unnecessarily at conferences and trade fairs.

- Remove your name from mailing lists if they provide you with nothing of value.

- Consider internal communications. Circulation lists within organizations are often unnecessarily large. If you can do so without creating political difficulties for yourself, ask to be taken off the circulation list for documents which do not concern you in any way.

- Examine subscriptions to periodicals. Those which have not yielded anything worthwhile in the last six months may be due for cancellation.

- If you have a secretary or assistant, get him or her to screen material before it gets to you. This is additional, not an alternative, to the other points on this list. Your secretary has no more reason to be burdened by junk mail than you have.

- Don't allow documents that will be routinely handled by members of your staff to be routed through you unless there is a good reason for it.

ORGANIZE YOUR DESK

I used to pretend that I could work well with a cluttered desk. Despite the various piles of paper, at times threatening to engulf the workspace, I claimed that I could easily put my hand on any document I needed and that shifting my attention from one task to another kept me sharp throughout my working day. It was nonsense, of course. Superfluous papers are a distraction from the job in hand in much the same way as interruptions and phone calls. It is all too easy to flit around a crowded desk, pecking at tasks rather than devoting the concentrated effort needed to complete them. Searching for documents you need can waste considerable amounts of time and throw up further distractions. Even if you resist the distractions, the presence of piles of paper representing dozens of tasks yet to be tackled, is a potent source of stress.

Move paperwork quickly in line with the five Ds outlined in Chapter 1.

Don't use your desk as filing space – use project folders or bring forward files for work in progress.

Keep items you use regularly close at hand.

Don't transfer piles of paper on your desk to piles of paper in other parts of the office.

You may need to overcome a psychological hurdle in clearing your desk. There is a tendency to associate the crowded desk with a busy owner, and we like to think of ourselves as busy. Remember, however, that one can be busy but incompetent and unproductive. Let the results of your activities speak for you rather than the appearance of your desk.

FILE SELECTIVELY

It has been estimated that 75 to 85 per cent of the material stored in filing cabinets is never referred to again. This represents a poor return on a major information handling task, and it is worth giving some thought to more effective filing strategies.

Filing is not a matter of getting a document off your desk when you're frightened to throw it away but are not sure what else to do with it. A document should only make it to the filing cabinet when it cannot be readily accessed elsewhere and there is a reasonable chance that it will be needed again in the future.

Effective filing requires:

- clarity about what is important;
- a consistent approach to what you intend to save and where you will put particular items;
- organization of material in such a way that allows rational expansion.

If somebody else does your filing for you, it is tempting to leave the whole tedious business to him or her. But remember that it is still your information, and it is worthwhile knowing the structure of the filing system so that when you mark a document for filing you are sending it to a known location rather than a black hole. This process of mentally slotting the document into place will assist your memory of its existence:

- File items according to the context in which they are likely to be sought.
- Keep a list of your files handy to avoid opening new files which overlap with those that already exist.
- Don't file hard copy of information already stored on computer. Ensure a sensible directory structure for your computer files with reliable back up. It is quicker to do, easier to find and amend, and takes up less room.
- Don't file material that is readily available from other sources such as the originator of the document, central archives, Internet reference sources.

Organizations are increasingly using shared document storage, often in an electronic form. These offer much more powerful search capabilities than manual systems – thus reducing the possibility of documents going missing. However, the very ease of recovery may still lead to the unnecessary storage of low value information.

PRUNE AND REORGANIZE PAPER STORAGE

When you are struggling to cope with a heavy information load, the idea of reorganizing and pruning your files may come fairly low on your list of priorities. But without regular attention files can rapidly become out of hand, and may exacerbate your overload. Even if you have somebody else to maintain your main files, it is likely that you have some personal files, and these can present a major problem when you are trying to put your hand on a document. Storage life varies according to the nature of the information. Some items become redundant in a matter of weeks, while others need to be kept for years. Weeding out what needs to be discarded or archived can be daunting.

Try a 'little and often' approach. Overhauling all your files is a job destined to be postponed indefinitely, but spending 5 or 10 minutes sorting a couple of files at the end of each day is eminently manageable. Be ruthless with the rubbish and don't allow yourself to get bogged down in spin-off tasks. If there are items which have been misplaced or one file needs to be merged with another, just put the items where they need to go, and resist the temptation to sort the destination file unless it is one you have already dealt with. Its turn will come in due course.

GET RID OF THE PILES

What about those piles of paper which have built up on your desk and around your office? The prospect of tackling them may be intimidating, but by setting aside some time for a disciplined blitz, you can get rid of them and lift the mental weight of their presence.

In addition to items which need action on your part or should be directed to others, it is likely that your paper piles will consist of documents (reports, periodicals, etc) which you have put aside to be read later, items which have not made it to the filing cabinet, and things which you were not sure what to do with.

Your objective is to get through the paper piles; you must not let yourself become bogged down. So, be prepared to attack the offending heaps and deal quickly and decisively with their contents.

Earmark four empty folders, filing trays or baskets and mark them: **Deal with, Distribute, Read, File**. Make sure you have sufficient plastic bin bags for the most important category – the discard pile.

Approach the task with the view that the majority of items are destined for the bin. Whatever relevance they had when they joined the pile is likely to have diminished. Don't repeat previous indecisiveness. If in doubt, throw it out.

Don't waste time reading items. Skim them to the point of determining whether they are needed and if so put them in the relevant tray or basket.

Don't file or act upon things as you go; you will become bogged down and distracted. By all means mark items to assist your actions and filing later, but keep to your main objective – to blast through the pile.

Zip through magazines and periodicals, tearing out the pages containing articles you wish to keep and throwing the rest away. Don't stop to read any of them at this stage.

When you have worked your way through the piles, turn your attention to the four trays. Schedule time to deal with the reading and filing tasks, and use your 'bring forward' system to determine when the 'deal with' items will be actioned.

Tackled in this way, a fearsome chore can become a real stress-buster.

4

WORK WITH OTHERS

There is only so much that you can do on your own. Your information load will be heavily influenced by the actions of colleagues, clients and suppliers. Bringing your influence to bear on them will require a mixture of assertiveness, diplomacy and trust.

OVERCOME DISTRACTIONS AND INTERRUPTIONS

Interruptions and distractions impose heavily on our ability to handle information. Not only is there the actual time lost through the interruption, but, more importantly, the effort of getting back to the original task and refocusing attention.

Some interruptions will occur for genuine business reasons, while others are more social, often by people who are themselves engaged in procrastination over tasks they want to escape. You may even be the source of the interruption. It is very easy to convince yourself that you just have to make a phone call or get a coffee, and that you will be back on the task in a few minutes. Once the pattern of work is disrupted, you find other pressing chores and the minutes stretch to an hour or more, after which time it is much harder to pick up the threads.

Dealing with interruptions and distractions requires firmness with yourself and others:

- If you are fortunate enough to have an assistant or secretary, get him or her to field phone calls and callers.

- If you don't have the benefit of an assistant, explore a reciprocal arrangement with colleagues whereby you divert your phone to others so that they can take messages for you when you need to work on a task uninterrupted. You, of course, do the same for them at other times.

- If this is not possible, disable the ringing tone on your phone and use voice mail or an answering machine to collect your messages. It helps in these circumstances to have another number which people can ring in the event of an urgent message.

- Set a regular time each day when you will deal with information-intensive tasks and will be unavailable for meetings, calls and other interruptions. Stick to it rigidly and others will come to recognize it.

- Be firm with self-generated interruptions. Recognize them as time-wasting habits.

- Help to foster a climate conducive to effective work by treating colleagues as you would have them treat you. Don't expect people to refrain from interrupting you, if you are in the habit of interrupting them.

- Take breaks at predetermined times.

- If an interruption is unavoidable, put a time limit on it. Let the person interrupting you know that you can only spare, say, five minutes.

- Risk being considered rude by not inviting interrupters to sit down.

- Close your door, if you have one.

AVOID ISSUING OVERLOAD INVITATIONS

'Leave it with me.' 'Let me have something in writing.' These are two of the easiest responses to make when a colleague brings you a proposal or problem and you are too busy or distracted to listen. You get rid of them without having to make a decision, but you have landed yourself with additional work. By inviting a colleague to leave an issue with you, not only do you have to spend time re-focusing on the matter, but you have also acquired responsibility for the next action, on a matter which may be outside your normal responsibilities.

Asking for something in writing may be valid if it is clear that the idea requires further work, or needs to be expressed on paper as part of a case to others. As a delaying tactic it results in unnecessary work for your colleague and a subsequent needless increase in your own information burden. It may also spawn further written communication on other issues.

INFLUENCE CLIENTS

Many organizations spend a great deal of time and effort keeping their clients informed of work in progress. From solicitors' letters detailing each step in the course of a house purchase, to outlines of work to date in a design project, the business of compiling progress reports can seriously detract from the effort required to complete the task in hand. Often clients do not need the level of interim information provided. They may just want to know that their work is on track and to have a ready response to queries, but the production of more elaborate material has become a standard ritual. Take care not to appear unwilling to provide clients with the detail they may have been used to in the past. Invite them to identify their own needs within the context of a drive towards more efficient communication. Given that overload is likely to be just as much a factor in your clients' lives as your own, a well-presented offer of simpler communication is likely to be well received.

PROVIDE ACCESSIBLE INFORMATION

Do you send people the information you think they may need, or locate it such that they can access it when required? The latter is obviously preferable in respect of reducing overload and the problem of information stored in multiple locations. Centrally located information must be accessible and reliable, and clearly people need to know that it exists. Computer networks provide the best mix of these three requirements. Even within small organizations it can be quite feasible to provide a bulletin board system and a database of shared documents. In the absence of an electronic system, centralized information can work well, but it is necessary for somebody to have the responsibility and resources for maintaining it. If your organization does not have a central arrangement, consider an agreement between colleagues that certain individuals will maintain and store particular types of information.

ENCOURAGE CHANGE

Time spent encouraging others to change their information habits should be repaid by a reduction in your own load. If you are in a senior position, you have an advantage in terms of introducing change. But take care not to send out mixed messages. Many managers like the idea of being freed from paperwork but still stop short of full delegation and empowerment of their staff. If staff are unsure of the boundaries of their responsibilities they will cling to the security which comes from over-informing their superiors.

Those in more junior positions are not necessarily powerless to bring about change. Use opportunities such as meetings, suggestion schemes and one-to-one discussions with your boss to introduce your proposals. Recognize that some managers will seek to justify their own position by keeping staff under pressure, or may consider it important that others go through the same rigours they had to endure as juniors.

Whatever your position, there are some simple ground rules if you are to win people over to your way of thinking:

- Look at the issue from the point of view of others. If people are to embrace change, it is important that they can see some benefit in it for themselves.

- However beneficial a change may be, there will be some who will resist it. Anticipate their objections and have persuasive responses ready.

- Costs or savings have a powerful impact in all areas of work. If you can work out a realistic estimate of savings, your proposals will be off to a good start.

- Take account of the prevailing organizational culture. Bureaucratic, hierarchical organizations have the most to gain from more effective handling of information, but tend to be the most resistant to change. Patience and perseverance are essential. You should be ready to accept small incremental steps achieved by working through established channels rather than expecting to achieve everything at one go.

● People most readily embrace change when they think that the impetus for it has come from themselves. Although it may seem an unnatural thing to do, resist the temptation to retain ownership of your ideas. Look for opportunities to credit others with a contribution to the initiative.

Co-operative campaigns and initiatives

The following are some ideas for raising awareness and reducing overload. If it is not possible to introduce such initiatives across the organization in which you work, significant results can be obtained within a department, section or group of colleagues. The ideas are not meant to be definitive, and you can probably think of adaptations or additions that are particularly appropriate to your working situation.

Recycling box: place a large cardboard box in a prominent position within a shared office. Over the course of a week, colleagues use it as a repository for all unnecessary paperwork received. As well as raising awareness, informal analysis of the contents can lead to agreement on ways to reduce needless documentation.

Return to sender campaign: agree that internal items received that have been sent unnecessarily will be returned to the sender. This has the advantage of giving the senders simple and direct feedback which allows them to rethink what they circulate to whom. However, the initiative needs to be presented carefully if it is not to be perceived by some as a snub to their efforts.

Simplify-a-form campaign: if over-complicated forms are a problem, agree a target number of revisions over a set period and apportion responsibility fairly across sections or departments.

Copying reductions: publish photocopier totals on a monthly basis and set targets for reductions.

Co-operative reading: colleagues agree to take it in turns to be the lead reader of weighty reports or new guidelines. He or she does the donkey work on a document and provides the others with a summary.

Communication policy: many organizations do not have a communication policy. Those that exist are often out of date, and may even encourage the proliferation of information. Agreeing or rethinking your communication policy is as important for the process of awareness raising as it is for the final outcome.

5

MANAGE ONLINE COMMUNICATION AND RESEARCH

COMMUNICATE EFFECTIVELY BY E-MAIL

E-mail is one of the simplest computer applications to use. Even a computer novice can master it in an hour or so. It is:

- **immediate**: you can tap out an e-mail message and deliver it to its destination in moments. Other documents, spreadsheets, diagrams, even video, can be sent as attachments provided the recipient has the appropriate software to open them.

- **informal**: forget about letter writing and memo conventions. With e-mail the basic memo structure is set up for you, and you don't need to worry about whether your communication fills the page. Three words are as acceptable as 300.

- **easy to file or discard**: provided that you have set up your system adequately, you can instantly file any e-mail message that it is important to save. Those that do not need to be kept are somehow easier to blast into oblivion by the fact that they do not appear on paper.

E-mail works in a similar fashion whether you are operating within a company network (Intranet) or across the globe (Internet). It is important, of course, to have other e-mail users to communicate with. If the majority of your contacts are not yet on e-mail, then gearing yourself up will not reap overload rewards. However, this is becoming increasingly unlikely as more and more people and organizations tap into the benefits of e-mail. The downside is that e-mail suffers from many of the same problems as paper, with the added dimension that the even greater ease of copying and transmission makes junk mail yet more prevalent.

HOW TO REDUCE E-MAIL OVERLOAD

- Make use of the time independence of e-mail. Just because it is an immediate communication medium doesn't mean that you have to deal with it immediately. Unlike telephone calls or other interruptions, e-mail (and voice mail for that matter) will sit in your in-box until you are ready to read it. An effective user will deal with it once or twice a day at a time when other tasks are not a priority.

- Don't spread your e-mail address around unnecessarily. It will attract junk e-mail.

- Treat your e-mail in-box in accordance with the five Ds for paper in-trays in Chapter 1 (discard, deal with, direct, deposit, determine future action).

- Don't worry about discarding items unread. If the header information suggests that an item is not worth reading, click the delete button. Waste no more time.

- Create suitably indexed folders to store any e-mail messages you wish to keep, so that you can easily find them again.

- Avoid over-copying to others if you want them to treat you in the same way.

- Promotional e-mail is normally generated automatically and sent to large mailing lists. There is often a simple response message that will take you off the list.

- When sending e-mails, indicate if you don't require an answer. Otherwise, people will often respond with just a brief addition to the original message; time-wasting for you to open and read.

- Report persistent junk mailers to your service provider, or use a junk mail filter such as the one in Microsoft Outlook.

OBTAIN USEFUL INFORMATION FROM THE INTERNET

In this section we are only concerned with the Internet as a source of information, and not its functions in terms of selling or entertainment. In the available space, it has to be assumed that you are already familiar to some degree with the main Internet vehicle, the World Wide Web. If you have not previously used the Internet, you may wish to consult another book in this series – *30 Minutes to Master the Internet.*

The main problem with the Internet is the sheer volume of information available. This presents three difficulties:

1. Separating the information you need from the mass of less relevant data;
2. Deciding when to stop searching;
3. Avoiding distractions.

HOW TO AVOID INTERNET OVERLOAD

The Internet is huge and invitingly accessible. You are just a couple of mouse clicks away from millions of pages of information, and the temptation is toward excessive searching for fear of missing some vital piece of information tucked away in the vast unruly collection. But resist the urge to seek information perfection. Nowhere does the 80: 20 rule apply more than on the Internet (80 per cent of the results come from 20 per cent of the effort), and you can waste large amounts of time chasing a rapidly diminishing addition to useful data. Concentrate, instead, on precise and well-planned searches that will get you quickly to manageable quantities of quality information.

Searching

Surfing – following links from one Web site to another – is the least effective way to locate specific information. You need to start by adopting an appropriate search vehicle. These can be classified as Internet Directories or Search Engines.

Internet directories such as Yahoo (www.yahoo.com) index sites under subject headings with progressively more specialized sub-headings. Approaching an information-gathering task via one of these is fine for general information or locating a specific site, but of limited value if what you are after is a specific reference that may be buried within a Web page. For this you will need to use a search engine such as AltaVista (www.altavista.com) or Infoseek (www.infoseek.com). These are compiled and updated using 'Web crawling' software which trawls the World Wide Web looking for new pages and scanning their entire content. Finding the information you want is a matter of choosing the best combination of keywords to pull the relevant pages out from millions of others.

There is increasing integration between Internet directories and search engines. Some employ both a subject-indexed directory and a comprehensive keyword search engine. In addition to searching the World Wide Web, some offer searches of Usenet. This consists of thousands of subject-specific news groups in which participants exchange information and views on topics of interest. Although a great deal of the content is garbage, some groups may serve to locate information not available elsewhere.

Here are some tips:

Take care in formulating your search request. If you enter keywords which are too general, you risk being deluged with thousands of pages of information. Search engines rank response to queries, with those that most nearly meet the search criteria at the top of the list, but a vague enquiry may throw up hundreds of responses with similar rankings. Some lateral thinking may be necessary in choosing keywords likely to be in the material you are seeking.

Use optional 'operators' to narrow your search. All search engines employ devices for more sophisticated searching. These vary slightly from one search engine to another. Check the help section of the search engine you are using; it will normally contain basic search tips as well as sophisticated ways of homing in on the information you require.

Don't let yourself be distracted by links to other interesting but irrelevant pages. If something attracts your interest, use the bookmark or favourite places facility to store a record of the location so that you can return to it at a later date.

Experiment with different search engines. Some are better than others for particular types of information. When you light upon one you like, make yourself familiar with its search conventions by looking up search tips in its help menu. Then use it as your regular first choice search vehicle.

If, despite careful definition of your search words, your first choice search engine fails to deliver the information you are looking for, try a different one. You may get a better result.

If you are already an advanced Internet user who regularly needs to use it as a research tool, you may benefit from using **a search assistant** or **offline browser**. The first of these is an application that can help you to organize and track your searches – sending the same query to different search engines if required. Offline browsers allow you to set standard queries and keep up to date with designated pages.

6

MAKE TECHNOLOGY WORK FOR YOU

Technology is both the cause of overload and a solution to it. Technologically assisted generation and communication of information have led to a huge increase in the volume of information in daily circulation. Far from achieving the paperless office envisaged in the early 1980s, ever larger quantities of paper are being produced, handled and stored. Add to that the increasing use of e-mail and the biggest information repository of all, the Internet, and you have the fundamentals of technology as villain of the piece. But the tremendous capacity of technology to assist us in creating, communicating, manipulating and storing information also offers potential solutions to the problem. Your success in this will depend on judicious choice and effective use of the available tools.

KNOW WHEN NOT TO USE TECHNOLOGY

Information technology has become so all pervading that one may be tempted to use it for every information-handling task. This would be a mistake. There are occasions when the effort of using technology outweighs the advantage, or the medium is inappropriate:

- producing a word-processed memo in response to an internal communication, when a simple hand-written note on the original document would suffice;

- setting up a computer database of contact phone numbers when your number of contacts is limited and likely to stay that way;

- using time and energy to learn a software package to carry out a function that could be performed manually and has only marginal or occasional significance in your workload.

CHOOSE APPROPRIATE SOFTWARE

Let genuine needs drive your software decisions. It is all too easy to be enticed by the productivity claims of a particular software package, and having acquired it, to look around for a task on which to use it. Using a product to meet an identified need is generally an effective way of learning it, but take care not to set yourself unrealistic timescales for achieving your targets with a new application.

Match the payoff in terms of improved productivity against the investment of time to become proficient in the application. Even if a package looks straightforward, allow plenty of time to get to grips with it. There may be unexpected glitches to overcome.

The value of particular packages will vary from person to person. It will be dependent on how much you have used other similar products; the way you like to work; and the precise nature of your job. Use magazine reviews and recommendations to aid your decision, but recognize that only you can make an accurate assessment of whether an application is worth having.

If you are new to computers

If you are new to computers, you should go initially for the easiest to learn general software without attempting to analyse your needs too deeply. You are likely to get the greatest initial information handling advantage by learning to use e-mail, a word processor and a Personal Information Manager.

The most common problems for new computer users are not knowing where to start, and fear of making disastrous mistakes. The first is a matter of taking one's courage in both hands and pitching in. To the novice everything may seem daunting, but each step forward makes the next one less difficult. Many computer operations have the same basic format. There are a host of good tutorials in book form or CD ROM. Once you have mastered the basics, nothing can beat tackling a real project for reinforcing and progressing your learning.

Conquering fear of making mistakes starts with the understanding that there is almost nothing irretrievable you can do from the keyboard short of pouring coffee into it. Take care to save your work regularly and even seemingly catastrophic situations can be salvaged. It is helpful if there is somebody experienced to call upon when the unpredictable does happen, as it surely will. There is usually a simple and easily executed solution. If you don't have expert assistance, resist the temptation to become angry, and approach the difficulty methodically, making use of the trouble-shooting section in your software manual or Windows help.

Don't try to learn too much at once. Get to grips with one package before moving on to the next. Most software is now based on Microsoft Windows and has very similar screen layout and commands. If you have mastered one package, you can easily transfer to the next your knowledge of the familiar features, and work to address those aspects that are different.

If you are an experienced computer user

Before embarking on a new application, try to arrive at a realistic assessment of the information-handling benefit set against the investment of time in learning to use it. One way of doing this is to predict the payback period.

Estimate the amount of time it will take you to become proficient in the package and the amount of time you expect its use to save you each week. Divide the first figure by the second to arrive at a payback period. For example, if it takes you 20 hours to learn a package that only saves you 30 minutes a week, the pay back period will be 40 weeks. In other words, it will be almost a year before you derive any time saving. In this situation, there are likely to be other time investments that will produce more immediate rewards.

Should I upgrade?

Whatever software package you choose, within a short time there is likely to be an upgrade version available, promising new features and greater information-handling effectiveness. Make the decision on whether to upgrade based on the following:

Do I need the new features? Few of us use all the features of an application. New ones may sound attractive, but if they don't offer you significant benefits there is no point in acquiring them.

Are the advantages worth the learning investment? Most upgraded packages will be broadly similar to their predecessors, but sometimes there is a major redesign that will require you to 'relearn' the application. Against this, the improvements may only be marginal. An upgrade may, from time to time, introduce new bugs or frustrations, or may run more slowly on your computer.

Do I need to review my computer habits?

The longer you have been using computers, the more likely this is to be the case. Experienced users may find that they are locked into ways of doing things that were learned when computers were slower and software less sophisticated; or that the trial and error way in which learning took place has bypassed important shortcuts. Half an hour revisiting the help file or manual of a software package or operating system may pay major dividends.

USEFUL TOOLS

In the space available, it is only possible to give an outline of some general software tools to assist in the management of information. Those which are specific to a particular area of work, eg accounts or design, are excluded, as are those where the primary purpose is with presentation of information.

Word processors

The word processor is the ubiquitous computer application and one of the simplest with which to be up and running quickly. Provided that you can navigate the keyboard, use the 'delete' and 'backspace' keys and the 'save' and 'print' functions, you can use the word processor at a basic level to create, store and amend documents. To produce attractive documents you will need to use some of the layout functions, but the standard templates that come with most word processors can do most of the work for you. In recent years word processors have developed greatly in both sophistication and ease of use. They offer a multiplicity of tools which the average user does not employ, such as the ability to incorporate pictures, charts and tables into documents, to perform simple calculations and to display revisions.

Do I need to use a word processor if I already have secretarial assistance?

The answer to this depends on the way you like to work. Many people find that they can rapidly dictate routine items, but need to see more complex material in print as they develop it. If this applies to you, then you may benefit from structuring your thoughts on the word processor. Most word processors have an outlining facility that allows you to build up your structure from headings and subheadings. You may wish to put the draft of a document together and then leave your secretary to work on layout and graphics. Alternatively, you may wish to type the more complex passages and dictate the rest.

Spreadsheets

Spreadsheets can store and manipulate any form of numerical information. If you have to keep track and make sense of financial or statistical data, then some time spent learning a spreadsheet package may be valuable. In recent years, spreadsheet software designers have made it much easier for the average user to perform quite complex calculations. Charts and graphs can be generated from spreadsheet data with a couple of mouse clicks. However, most new users find spreadsheets a little trickier to learn than word processors.

Personal information managers

These are customized databases for storing and tracking personal information. Various applications fall into this category including such packages as Lotus Organiser, Starfish Sidekick and Microsoft Schedule+ and Outlook. A personal information manager is generally included with the major integrated office suites. Typical contents are:

- an address book to manage contacts;

- an appointments scheduler, which may be integrated with the address book or with a monthly or annual time planner, and which offers a reminder facility;

- 'to do' lists which can be arranged under subject headings and may permit some simple project planning in terms of target date, planned duration, etc;

- recording of time spent on activities and expenses tracking;

- free note space which may be adapted to particular purposes, and generally allows importation of information from other packages.

Packages such as Microsoft Outlook will also help you to manage your e-mails and to incorporate them within your schedules and 'to do' lists. Where personal information managers are set up on company-wide networks, they can greatly assist in the scheduling of meetings, provided that the majority of people take the trouble to put their personal schedules on the system.

Pocket organizers and personal digital assistants

These hardware devices range from simple electronic address books to full-blown hand-held PCs. In the mid-range you will get most of the features of a PIM software package (address book, calendar, scheduler, reminder, notes) in an easily pocketable device. At the high end, you will also get cut-down versions of standard word processing, spreadsheet and communications software. The downside with these machines is that they have small keyboards and are inconvenient for large-scale data input. Also, despite facilities for file transfer between your PDA and desktop computer, it can be a nuisance to synchronize data on different systems.

Project management software

Specialist project management software such as Microsoft Project is very powerful and is capable of allocating and tracking tasks and resources across several complex projects simultaneously. If you are going to make full use of such facilities you will benefit from some knowledge of project management conventions, and you will need to invest some time into learning the product. There are other more basic programs available, including some quite good packages that can be downloaded from the Internet. If you simply want to track personal projects and assignments for a small number of others you may well find that the scheduling facilities of a Personal Information Manager will be adequate for your needs.

Voice recognition software

With a voice recognition package you can dictate material via a microphone and the computer will convert it into text. There are a number of products available. Some allow you to work with your normal word processor, while others have their own text editor, from which you can paste text into your word processor. Early packages required the separate enunciation of each word in a manner that is difficult to achieve when speaking naturally. However, the software has developed to a point where it can now cope with more normal speech, and producers claim up to 95 per cent accuracy with speeds of up to 140 words per minute. Experience suggests that some of these claims may be a little optimistic. To make use of a voice recognition package your computer will need a reasonably fast processor and plenty of memory. Check the minimum specifications before buying. You should be prepared to spend some time 'training' the package to recognize your particular speech patterns and correcting a significant number of mistakes which will occur before the package becomes used to your voice.

Electronic filing systems

In addition to the appropriate software, electronic filing of information originated on paper requires two hardware elements: a means of getting documents into the computer (scanner), and a large-scale storage device. Until quite recently, both were expensive and such systems could not be considered by many companies. Now, relatively inexpensive solutions make this an option for organizations of all sizes. Larger enterprises may have a central document processing and archiving system, but even the smallest company or self-employed individual can set up a simple filing system using a scanner and a writable CD ROM drive. Such devices now retail very cheaply, and frequently come with free document filing software. CDs can store large quantities of material and, with the rewritable variety, it is possible to store and delete information many times over almost as simply as using a floppy disc. Some software will allow you to store all types of files together – scanned documents, word processor and spreadsheet files, and e-mails or documents downloaded from the Internet. All may be accessed in a flash using subject category, keywords or date filed. Remember, however, that putting paper documents into the system still takes time, and so you should not use an electronic filing system as an excuse for abandoning any discrimination about what gets filed and what thrown away.

Keyboard training packages

If you are a two-finger typist who does a significant amount of keyboard work, you may benefit from the increase in typing speed which follows from developing the use of all your fingers. There are a number of inexpensive keyboard trainers available on CD ROM which take you through staged development and practice. It is not unreasonable to look for a doubling of your speed with 8 to 12 hours of work. If you have been typing with two fingers for a long time, then you might find it a little more difficult to make the change, but as a former two-finger typist of 30 years standing, I can testify that the change is possible with a little perseverance, and makes a considerable difference to productivity.

7

IF YOU ARE STILL OVERLOADED

Despite your best endeavours with the overload-beating suggestions in this book, it may be that you simply have a job with an information load too large for one person to handle. The job you do may have grown or, as is increasingly common in a climate dominated by restructuring and downsizing, you may have found yourself with a workload previously covered by two. While it might have been the intention that certain things would give way to allow you to take on the additional work, the unfortunate reality is that you are generally expected to maintain all the original communication channels, and others count on receiving the same level of service as they enjoyed previously.

In circumstances where effective management of your information load is not enough, you either grit your teeth and soldier on – this may be the only option if everybody else is under the same pressure – or you take steps to relinquish responsibilities or obtain additional help.

Before embarking on the second course of action you should make sure that you have exhausted such workload distribution options as are reasonably in your power. For example, have you used opportunities to delegate and done so appropriately – giving responsibility and authority to the other person? You should also prepare your case well, if you are to be successful. Here are some tips:

- Choose an appropriate time to raise your request with your boss, preferably not when either of you are under pressure or distracted by other events.

- Be clear about the important goals and priorities in your job, and attempt to identify accurately the particular information demands which are leading to overload.

- Avoid a presentational style that is either confrontational or apologetic.

- Make sure that you are able to articulate lucid and achievable solutions to the problems you have identified.

- Take care to avoid any misinterpretation of your motives, for example, the impression that you are just trying to shed what you don't like.

- Look at the situation from the point of view of the person to whom you are taking the problem. It will help you to put your argument in a manner with which he or she can identify.

- Think in advance about your compromise position, in the event that you are not able to achieve everything that you seek.

8

SUMMARY AND ACTION PLAN

In 30 minutes we have looked at the major causes of information overload, and strategies for overcoming it. You will need to spend a little longer, once you have put the book down, if you are going to make these strategies work for you. Awareness and good intentions are not enough to put you in control of your information load. You will need a systematic approach to implementing those strategies you consider important, and some method of review if you are to avoid the tendency to drift back to old habits – something which those under pressure from a busy schedule are particularly prone to do.

The following summary and action plan aim to help you build a personal strategy that will make a permanent change to your way of working:

1. Identify, from the list, those elements that offer you potential benefit.

2. Next, allocate a letter from A to C to indicate the priority you attach to the item. (A = highest priority.)

3. Set a date by which you will have achieved, or will review progress towards, those items you have identified as priority A. You may wish to give a date to priority B and C also, but beware of tackling too much at once.

Some items are of a one-off nature and can have a firm date set for achievement. Others require an ongoing effort to change your own habits and exert influence on other people. For these a realistic progress review date is needed.

STEPS TO BETTER INFORMATION HANDLING

Action	Priority	Review date
Eliminate fear habits		
Tackle procrastination		
Work on identifying important information		
Adopt the 5Ds approach		
Increase reading speed		
Introduce other good reading habits		
Improve concentration		
Develop memory habits		
Reduce paper inflow		

Action	Priority	Review date
Organize desk space		
Introduce better filing habits		
Prune or reorganize existing files		
Tackle paper piles		
Overcome distractions and interruptions		
Dispel overload invitations		
Influence clients		
Provide accessible information		
Encourage others to change		
Manage e-mail effectively		
Get the best from the Internet		
Choose appropriate software solutions		
Learn new software packages		
1.		
2.		
3.		
4.		
Negotiate a change in workload